Does God Desire
All to Be Saved?

Does God Desire All to Be Saved?

John Piper

WHEATON, ILLINOIS

This book is a revised and expanded version of material previously published in: Thomas R. Schreiner and Bruce A. Ware, eds., *The Grace of God, the Bondage of the Will: Biblical and Practical Perspectives on Calvinism* (Grand Rapids: Baker, 1995); Thomas R. Schreiner and Bruce A. Ware, eds., *Still Sovereign: Contemporary Perspectives on Election, Foreknowledge, and Grace* (Grand Rapids: Baker, 2000); and John Piper, *The Pleasures of God: Meditations on God's Delight in Being God*, revised edition (Sisters, OR: Multnomah, 2000).

First printing 2013

Printed in the United States of America

Trade paperback ISBN: 978-1-4335-3719-6
Mobipocket ISBN: 978-1-4335-3721-9
PDF ISBN: 978-1-4335-3720-2
ePub ISBN: 978-1-4335-3722-6

Library of Congress Cataloging-in-Publication Data

Piper, John, 1946-
   Does God desire all to be saved? / John Piper.
      pages   cm
   Includes bibliographical references and index.
   ISBN 978-1-4335-3719-6 (tp)
     1. Election (Theology) 2. Salvation—Christianity.
3. Universalism. I. Title.
BT810.3.P575   2013
232—dc23   2013014374

Crossway is a publishing ministry of Good News Publishers.

VP		23	22	21	20	19	18	17	16	15	14	13
15	14	13	12	11	10	9	8	7	6	5	4	3	2	1

To

Tom Schreiner and Bruce Ware,
humble partners in handling
the Word of Truth

Contents

Introduction

When climbing from lowlands to mountaintops, one must often pass through clouds. That's the way it has been for me all my life as I have tried to get the best views of the glory of God.

When you enter a layer of clouds, it helps to have a guide to keep you away from the precipices and on the path to the other side of the murkiness. That's one way to view this book. I hope it will serve as a guide upward through the haze and confusion about God's electing and saving will.

I admit that some of the paths in this book are steep. And some of the steepest places are through the thickest clouds. The climb is not for everyone. We all have different gifts, and not everyone is called to this kind of intellectual climb. I don't mean that the non-climbers will see less glory or worship with less passion. There are glories in the valleys. And there are paths into beauties of God that are less intellectual. I would not dare to claim that those who do this sort of climbing always see or savor more glory than those with wider eyes for the glory that is right there in the meadow.

Nevertheless, some of us are wired to make this climb. There is not much choice in it. We should no more boast about doing it than one should boast about being a morning person. Almost every time we open our Bibles, we see challenges. Puzzles. Mysteries. Paradoxes. Mountain paths beckon us, but seem to lead in opposite directions. We move toward these paths like bumblebees toward morning glories.

So if you are like me in this way, I would like to invite you to take a climb. I don't claim to be superior, but it may be that on this mountain I've gone up and down enough times to be of some help. There are clouds. It can get really murky on the way to the brightness on the other side. I would like to help if I can.

The paths that beckon us on this mountain are the path of God's election and the path of God's will for all people to be saved. Election seems to say that God has a people who are his, and he sees to it that they come to Christ and are saved. But the other path seems to say that God loves everyone and invites everyone to come, and wants them all to be saved.

On the mountain path of election, Jesus says: "I have manifested your name to the people whom you gave me out of the world. Yours they were, and you gave them to me, and they have kept your word" (John 17:6). And in another place, he says, "No one can come to me unless it is granted him by the Father" (John 6:65). Or, as God says in Romans 9:15, "I will have mercy on whom I have mercy, and I will have compassion on whom I have compassion." Then Paul draws out the inference: "So then it depends not on human will or exertion, but on God, who has mercy" (v. 16).

But on the mountain path of God's desire for all, Jesus says to the city that is about to kill him: "O Jerusalem, Jerusalem, the city that kills the prophets and stones those who are sent to it! How often would I have gathered your children together as a hen gathers her brood under her wings, and you were not willing!" (Luke 13:34). And he offers an open and free invitation to everyone who is heavy laden, thirsty, and perishing: "Come to me, all who labor and are heavy laden, and I will give you rest" (Matt. 11:28); "If anyone thirsts, let him come to me and drink" (John 7:37); "For God so loved the world, that he gave his only Son, that whoever believes in him should not perish but have eternal life" (John 3:16).

It's an old paradox. I didn't climb this mountain by myself.

More seasoned climbers than I helped me along the way. I'll introduce them to you as we go.

The aim of the climb is not intellectual satisfaction. The aim is worship. God gets more honor when we worship on the basis of what we know about him than he gets if we worship on the basis of what we don't know. If our effort to know God more clearly is not an effort to love him more dearly, it will be fatal. "'Knowledge' puffs up, but love builds up" (1 Cor. 8:1). This means that the only knowledge worth having in the end is knowledge that leads to love—love for God and love for people.

This leads to a second aim of this climb: missions and ministry. The aim of knowing is loving people—all the peoples of the world and all the people in the neighborhood. If we are confused about God's election and God's universal invitation to salvation, we will not love the world as we ought.

These are dangerous and difficult days in world missions. Hundreds of unreached peoples that Jesus commands us to evangelize belong to religions and cultures that do not want us to come to them. But Jesus did not say, "Go make disciples where you are wanted." He said, "I am sending you out as lambs in the midst of wolves" (Luke 10:3). Without a clear, strong conviction about God's saving will for these peoples, we will not have the resolve to go.

The same is true of our neighborhoods, near as well as far. There is suburban misery no money can heal. The brokenness may be hidden, but it is real. The rich are perishing. Most of them do not want us to tell them all is not well.

And in the ever-multiplying poor urban centers of the world, the pain, brokenness, sickness, dysfunction, hopelessness, and rage seem to be resistant to every kind of remedy. But Christians lean toward need, not comfort. At least we should. And the aim of this book is to bring such clarity to the will of God for ourselves and for the lost that we will not waver in moving toward need with the gospel of Christ.

God is sending us—all of us, in one way or another—to the world. We are not our own. We were bought with a price. We belong to Christ. His design for the world is our destiny. We have an inestimable treasure for the world—the gospel of Jesus Christ. We do not deserve it any more than they do. <u>That God has chosen us to know him and love him makes us debtors to every person.</u> If this book succeeds in helping you make it through the clouds of confusion to the light of God's glorious saving will, the evidence will be that you give yourself as never before to spreading this news:

> Come, everyone who thirsts,
>   come to the waters;
> and he who has no money,
>   come, buy and eat!
> Come, buy wine and milk
>   without money and without price. (Isa. 55:1)

We implore you on behalf of Christ, be reconciled to God. (2 Cor. 5:20)

1

My Aim

My aim in this short book is to show from Scripture that the simultaneous existence of God's will for all people to be saved and his will to choose some people for salvation unconditionally before creation[1] is not a sign of divine schizophrenia or exegetical confusion. A corresponding aim is to show that unconditional election therefore does not contradict biblical expressions of God's compassion for all people and does not rule out sincere offers of salvation to all who are lost among the peoples of the world.

The Perplexing Texts

First Timothy 2:4, 2 Peter 3:9, Ezekiel 18:23, and Matthew 23:37 are the texts most commonly cited to show that God's will is for all people to be saved and none to be lost.

- In 1 Timothy 2:1–4, Paul says that the reason we should pray for kings and all in high positions is that this may bring about a quiet and peaceable life that "is pleasing in the sight of God our Savior, who desires all people to be saved and to come to the knowledge of the truth."

[1] Matt. 22:14; John 6:37, 44, 65; 8:47; 10:26–29; Rom. 8:29–30; 9:6–23; 11:5–10; 1 Cor. 1:26–30; Eph. 1:4–5; 1 Thess. 1:4; 2 Thess. 2:13; James 2:5.

- In 2 Peter 3:8–9, the apostle says that the delay of the second coming of Christ is owing to the fact that with the Lord one day is as a thousand years and a thousand years is as a day: "The Lord is not slow to fulfill his promise as some count slowness, but is patient toward you, not wishing that any should perish, but that all should reach repentance."

- In Ezekiel 18:23 and 32, the Lord speaks about his heart for the perishing: "Have I any pleasure[2] in the death of the wicked, declares the Lord God, and not rather that he should turn from his way and live? . . . I have no pleasure in the death of anyone, declares the Lord God; so turn, and live."

- In Matthew 23:37, Jesus says: "O Jerusalem, Jerusalem, the city that kills the prophets and stones those who are sent to it! How often would I have gathered your children together as a hen gathers her brood under her wings, and you were not willing!"

It is possible that careful interpretation of 1 Timothy 2:4 would lead us to believe that God's *desire for all people to be saved* does not refer to every individual person in the world, but rather to all *sorts* of people, since "all people" in verse 1 may well mean groups such as "kings and all who are in high positions" (v. 2).[3] It is also possible that the "you" in 2 Peter 3:9 ("the Lord is . . . patient toward *you*, not wishing that any should perish") refers not to every person in the world but to professing Christians, among whom, as Adolf Schlatter says, "are people who only through repentance can attain to the grace of God and to the promised inheritance."[4]

---

[2] The emphatic doubling of the infinitive absolute with the finite verb for "have pleasure" is another way of expressing the oath in Ezekiel 33:11: "As I live, declares the Lord God, I have no pleasure in the death of the wicked." The intensification in the King James Version wording of Ezekiel 18:23, "Have I any pleasure *at all* that the wicked should die?" is not necessarily implied in the original Hebrew. The intensification of God's denial of *having pleasure* is to stress that he absolutely means what he says, not that the absence of every possible form of pleasure is absolute—as we will see later in the book.

[3] John Gill, *The Cause of God and Truth* (1735–1738; repr., London: W. H. Collingridge, 1855), 49–52.

[4] Adolf Schlatter, *Die Briefe des Petrus, Judas, Jakobus, der Brief an die Hebraeer, Erläuterungen zum Neuen Testament*, vol. 9 (Stuttgart: Calver Verlag, 1964), 126. This is especially true in view of v. 15, which urges the readers themselves to "count the patience of our Lord as salvation," and in view

Nevertheless, the case for this limitation on God's universal saving will has never been convincing to Arminians.[5] And for our purposes, this case is not decisive, since other texts are more compelling. Ezekiel 18:23, 32; 33:11; and Matthew 23:37 surely point to God's desire that all people be saved. Therefore, as a hearty believer in unconditional, individual election, I also rejoice to affirm that there is a real sense in which God does not take pleasure in the perishing of the impenitent, that he desired to gather all the rebellious inhabitants of Jerusalem, and that he has compassion on all people. My aim is to show that this is not double talk.

My purpose is not to defend the doctrine that God chooses unconditionally whom he will save. I have tried to do that elsewhere,[6] and others have done it more extensively than I.[7] Nevertheless, I will try to make a credible case that while the texts cited above may indeed be pillars for God's universal love and universal saving desire, they are not weapons against unconditional election.

---

of the fact that the delay of the second coming seems to result not in more individuals being saved worldwide, but in more being lost as the love of many grows cold (Matt. 24:12).

[5] Arminians have their name from Jacobus Arminius, who lived from 1560 to 1609. Their theology is usually contrasted with Reformed theology (or Calvinism) within the larger evangelical camp. With the Reformed, Arminians believe that humanity is fallen and unable to save itself. God must give prevenient grace to make us able to believe. But unlike the Reformed, Arminians do not believe that this prevenient grace is *decisive* in bringing about personal salvation, but rather that humans have the power of decisive self-determination, and that is what finally determines who is saved and who is not. Another doctrinal distinctive is summed up in *The Global Dictionary of Theology*: "For Arminius, predestination, instead of being unconditionally founded in God's will alone, is conditional on an individual's faith. God elects those to salvation who do not resist, but accept, his gracious gift of faith and perseverance; God reprobates those who stubbornly refuse to receive his saving gift." Thus, persevering to the end in faith and being saved is not certain. Christians can use their power of self-determination to reject the faith and lose their salvation (K. D. Stanglin, "Arminianism," in *The Global Dictionary of Theology*, ed. William A. Dyrness and Veli-Matti Kärkkäinen [Downers Grove, IL: InterVarsity Press, 2008], 61. See Roger E. Olson, *Arminian Theology* [Downers Grove, IL: InterVarsity Press, 2006]).

[6] See especially *The Justification of God: An Exegetical and Theological Study of Romans 9:1–23* (Grand Rapids: Baker, 1993); *The Pleasures of God: Meditations on God's Delight in Being God*, 3rd ed. (Colorado Springs: Multnomah, 2012), 33–59, 105–39; "How does a Sovereign God Love?" *Reformed Journal* 33, no. 4 (April 1983), 9–13; "Universalism in Romans 9–11? Testing the Exegesis of Thomas Talbott," *Reformed Journal* 33, no. 7 (July 1983), 1114.

[7] Thomas Schreiner, "Does Romans 9 Teach Individual Election unto Salvation?" in *Still Sovereign: Contemporary Perspectives on Election, Foreknowledge, and Grace*, eds. Thomas R. Schreiner and Bruce A. Ware (Grand Rapids: Baker, 2000), 89–106; Robert W. Yarborough, "Divine Election in the Gospel of John," in *Still Sovereign*, 47–62; Donald J. Westblade, "Divine Election in the Pauline Literature," in *Still Sovereign*, 63–88; Samuel Storms, *Chosen for Life: The Case for Divine Election* (Wheaton, IL: Crossway, 2007); R. C. Sproul, *Chosen by God: Knowing God's Perfect Plan for His Glory and His Children* (Carol Stream, IL: Tyndale, 2010).

Naming the Ways God Wills

Affirming the will of God to save *all*, while also affirming the unconditional election of *some*, implies that there are at least "two
wills" in God, or two ways of willing. It implies that God decrees
one state of affairs while also willing and teaching that a different
state of affairs should come to pass.

This distinction in the ways God wills is not a new contrivance.
It has been expressed in various ways throughout the centuries. For
example, theologians have spoken of "sovereign will" and "moral
will," "efficient will" and "permissive will," "secret will" and "revealed will," "will of decree" and "will of command," "decretive
will" and "preceptive will," and "*voluntas signi* (will of sign)" and
"*voluntas beneplaciti* (will of good pleasure)," among other terms.[8]

Criticism of the Two Wills in God

Clark Pinnock referred disapprovingly to "the exceedingly para-
doxical notion of two divine wills regarding salvation."[9] In Pinnock's edited volume, *A Case for Arminianism*, Randall G.
Basinger argues that "if God has decreed all events, then it must be
that things *cannot* and *should* not be any different from what they
are."[10] In other words, he rejects the notion that God could decree
that a thing be one way and yet teach that we should act to make it
another way. He says that it is too hard "to coherently conceive of
a God in which this distinction really exists."[11]

In the same volume, Fritz Guy argues that the revelation of
God in Christ has brought about a "paradigm shift" in the way
we should think about the love of God—namely, as "more funda-

---

[8] See Heinrich Heppe, *Reformed Dogmatics* (1860; repr., Grand Rapids: Baker, 1978), 143–49 for
the way the sixteenth- and seventeenth-century Reformed theologians talked about the relationship
between God's decrees and his moral law.

[9] Clark H. Pinnock, *Grace Unlimited* (Minneapolis: Bethany Fellowship, Inc., 1975), 13.

[10] Randall G. Basinger, "Exhaustive Divine Sovereignty: A Practical Critique," in *A Case for Arminianism: The Grace of God, the Will of Man*, gen. ed. Clark H. Pinnock (Grand Rapids: Zondervan,
1989), 196 (emphasis in original).

[11] Ibid., 203.

mental than, and prior to, justice and power." This shift, he says, makes it possible to think about the "will of God" as "delighting more than deciding." God's will is not his sovereign purpose that he infallibly establishes, but rather "the desire of the lover for the beloved." The will of God is his general intention and longing, not his effective purpose. Guy goes so far as to say, "Apart from a predestinarian presupposition, it becomes apparent that God's 'will' is always to be understood in terms of intention and desire [as opposed to efficacious, sovereign purpose]."[12]

These criticisms are not new. Jonathan Edwards wrote two hundred and fifty years ago: "The Arminians ridicule the distinction between the secret and revealed will of God, or, more properly expressed, the distinction between the decree and the law of God; because we say he may decree one thing, and command another. And so, they argue, we hold a contrariety in God, as if one will of his contradicted another."[13]

Driven by Texts, Not Logic

But in spite of these criticisms, the distinction stands, not because of a logical or theological deduction or necessity, but because it is inescapable in the Scriptures. The most careful exegete writing in Pinnock's *A Case for Arminianism* concedes the existence of two wills in God. I. Howard Marshall applies his exegetical gift to the Pastoral Epistles. Concerning 1 Timothy 2:4, he says:

> To avoid all misconceptions it should be made clear at the outset that the fact that God wishes or wills that all people should be saved does not necessarily imply that all will respond to the

---

[12] Fritz Guy, "The Universality of God's Love," in *A Case for Arminianism*, 35.

[13] Jonathan Edwards, "Concerning the Decrees in General, and Election in Particular," in *The Works of Jonathan Edwards*, vol. 2 (Edinburgh: The Banner of Truth Trust, 1974), 526. Of course, the theological distinction between two kinds of willing in God goes back much further. In the fourth part of his book *The Cause of God and Truth* (see note 3), John Gill gives one hundred double-columned pages of references from the early fathers (from Clement to Jerome) concerning this and other "Reformed" distinctives.

gospel and be saved. *We must certainly distinguish between what God would like to see happen and what he actually does will to happen, and both of these things can be spoken of as God's will.* The question at issue is not whether all will be saved but whether God has made provision in Christ for the salvation of all, provided that they believe, and without limiting the potential scope of the death of Christ merely to those whom God knows will believe.[14]

In this book, I would like to undergird Marshall's point that "we must certainly distinguish between what God would like to see happen and what he actually does will to happen, and [that] both of these things can be spoken of as God's will." Perhaps the most effective way to do this is to begin by drawing attention to the way Scripture portrays God's willing something in one sense that he disapproves in another sense. Then, after seeing some of the biblical evidence, we can step back and ponder how to understand it in relation to God's saving purposes.

---

[14] I. Howard Marshall, "Universal Grace and Atonement in the Pastoral Epistles," in *A Case for Arminianism*, 56 (emphasis added). One of the serious weaknesses of the argument in Marshall's chapter is the omission of any discussion or even mention of 2 Timothy 2:24–26, which says: "The Lord's servant must not be quarrelsome but kind to everyone, able to teach, patiently enduring evil, correcting his opponents with gentleness. *God may perhaps grant them repentance leading to a knowledge of the truth*, and they may come to their senses and escape from the snare of the devil, after being captured by him to do his will." Marshall asks whether any text in the Pastorals would lead us to believe that "faith and repentance are the gifts of God, who gives them only to the previously chosen group of the elect" (66). He concludes that there is not, even though he passes over the text that comes closest to saying this very thing (2 Tim. 2:25). The text is even more significant because its wording is used in 1 Timothy 2:4. Compare the desire of God for people to "be saved and to come to the knowledge of the truth" (1 Tim. 2:4) with the gift of God that people repent, "leading to a knowledge of the truth" (2 Tim. 2:25). These two texts alone probably teach that there are "two wills" in God: the will that all be saved and the will to give repentance to some.

2

Illustrations of Two Wills in God

The simple purpose of this chapter is to assemble biblical illustrations of God's two wills. What passages of Scripture portray God as willing something in one sense that he disapproves in another sense? We will focus on five biblical examples.

1. The Death of Christ

The most compelling example of God's willing for sin to come to pass while at the same time disapproving the sin is his willing the death of his perfect, divine Son. The betrayal of Jesus by Judas was a morally evil act inspired immediately by Satan (Luke 22:3). Yet, in Acts 2:23, Peter says, "This Jesus [*was*] *delivered up according to the definite plan and foreknowledge of God.*" The betrayal was sin, and it involved the instrumentality of Satan, but it was part of God's ordained plan. That is, there is a sense in which God willed the delivering up of his Son, even though Judas's act was sin.

Moreover, Herod's contempt for Jesus (Luke 23:11), the Jews' cry, "Crucify, crucify him!" (v. 21), Pilate's spineless expediency (v. 24), and the Gentile soldiers' mockery (v. 36) were also sinful attitudes and deeds. Yet in Acts 4:27–28, Luke expresses his understanding of the sovereignty of God in these acts by recording the prayer of the Jerusalem saints:

> Truly in this city there were gathered together against your holy servant Jesus, whom you anointed, both Herod and Pontius Pilate, along with the Gentiles and the peoples of Israel, to do *whatever your hand and your plan had predestined to take place.*

Herod, the Jewish crowds, Pilate, and the soldiers lifted their hands to rebel against the Most High, only to find that their rebellion was, in fact, unwitting (sinful) service in the inscrutable designs of God.

The appalling death of Christ was the will and work of God the Father. Isaiah writes, "We esteemed him stricken, *smitten by God. . . . It was the will of the* LORD *to crush him; he has put him to grief*" (Isa. 53:4, 10). God's will was very much engaged in the events that brought his Son to death on the cross. God considered it "fitting . . . [to] make the founder of their salvation perfect through suffering" (Heb. 2:10). Yet, as Jonathan Edwards points out, Christ's suffering "could not come to pass but by sin. For contempt and disgrace was one thing he was to suffer."[1]

It goes almost without saying that God wills obedience to his moral law, and that he wills this in a way that can be rejected by many. This is evident from numerous texts: "Not everyone who says to me, 'Lord, Lord,' will enter the kingdom of heaven, but the one who does *the will of my Father* who is in heaven" (Matt. 7:21); "Whoever does *the will of my Father* in heaven is my brother and sister and mother" (12:50); "Whoever does *the will of God* abides forever" (1 John 2:17). "The will of God" in these texts is the revealed, moral instruction of the Old and New Testaments, which forbids sin.

---

[1] Jonathan Edwards, "Concerning the Decrees in General, and Election in Particular," in *The Works of Jonathan Edwards*, vol. 2 (Edinburgh: The Banner of Truth Trust, 1974), 534.

Therefore, we know it was *not* the "will of God" that Judas, Herod, the Jewish crowds, Pilate, and the Gentile soldiers disobeyed the moral law of God by sinning in delivering Jesus up to be crucified. But we also know that it *was* the will of God that this should come to pass. Therefore, we know that God wills in one sense what he does not will in another sense. I. Howard Marshall's statement, quoted in chapter 1, is confirmed by the death of Jesus: "We must certainly distinguish between what God would like to see happen and what he actually does will to happen."[2]

2. The War against the Lamb

There are two reasons that we turn next to the book of Revelation. One is that the war against the Son of God, which reached its sinful climax at the cross, comes to final consummation in a way that confirms what we have seen about the will of God. The other reason is that this text reveals John's understanding of God's active involvement in fulfilling prophecies in ways that involve sinning. John sees a vision of some final events of history:

> And the ten horns that you saw, they and the beast will hate the prostitute. They will make her desolate and naked, and devour her flesh and burn her up with fire, for God has put it into their hearts to carry out his purpose by being of one mind and handing over their royal power to the beast, until the words of God are fulfilled. (Rev. 17:16–17)

Even without going into all the details of this passage, the relevant matter is clear. The beast rises from "the bottomless pit" (Rev. 17:8). He is the personification of evil and rebellion against God. The ten horns are ten kings (v. 12), and they "make war on the Lamb" (v. 14).

---

[2]I. Howard Marshall, "Universal Grace and Atonement in the Pastoral Epistles," in *A Case for Arminianism: The Grace of God, the Will of Man,* gen. ed. Clark H. Pinnock (Grand Rapids: Zondervan, 1989), 56.

Waging war against the Lamb is sin, and sin is contrary to the will of God. Nevertheless, the angel says (literally), "God has put it into their [the ten kings'] hearts *to carry out his purpose* by being of one mind and handing over their royal power to the beast, until the words of God are fulfilled" (v. 17). Therefore, God wills (in one sense) to influence the hearts of the ten kings so that they will do what is against his will (in another sense).

Moreover, God does this in fulfillment of prophetic words. The ten kings will collaborate with the beast "until the words of God are fulfilled." This implies something crucial about John's understanding of the fulfillment of "the prophecies leading up to the overthrow of Antichrist."[3] It implies that (at least in John's view) God's prophecies are not mere predictions about what God knows will happen, but rather are divine intentions that he makes sure will happen. We know this because verse 17 says that *God is acting* to see to it that the ten kings will make league with the beast "until the words of God are fulfilled." John is not exulting in the marvelous foreknowledge of God to predict a bad event. Rather, he is exulting in the marvelous sovereignty of God to make sure that the bad event comes about. Fulfilled prophecy, in John's mind, is not only prediction, but also promised divine performance.

This is important because John tells us in his Gospel that there are Old Testament prophecies of events surrounding the death of Christ that involve sin. This means that God intends to bring about events that involve things he forbids. These events include Judas's betrayal of Jesus (John 13:18; Ps. 41:9), the hatred Jesus received from his enemies (John 15:25; Pss. 69:4; 35:19), the casting of lots for Jesus's clothing (John 19:24; Ps. 22:18), and the piercing of Jesus's side (John 19:36–37; Ex. 12:46; Ps. 34:20; Zech. 12:10). John expresses his theology of God's sovereignty with these words: "These things took place *that* the Scripture might be fulfilled"

---

[3] Robert H. Mounce, *The Book of Revelation* (Grand Rapids: Eerdmans, 1977), 320. Mounce is following Isbon Beckwith, *The Apocalypse of John* (1919; repr., Grand Rapids: Baker, 1967), 703.

(John 19:36). In other words, the events were not a coincidence that God merely foresaw, but a plan that God *purposed* to bring about.[4] Thus, again we find Marshall's words confirmed: "We must certainly distinguish between what God would like to see happen and what he actually does will to happen."

3. The Hardening Work of God

Another evidence that demonstrates God's willing (in one sense) a state of affairs that he disapproves (in another sense) is the testimony of Scripture that God wills to harden some men's hearts so that they become obstinate in sinful behavior that he disapproves.

The best-known example is the hardening of Pharaoh's heart.[5] In Exodus 8:1, the Lord says to Moses, "Go in to Pharaoh and say to him, 'Thus says the LORD, "Let my people go, that they may serve me."'" In other words, God's command, that is, his *will*, was that Pharaoh let the Israelites go. Nevertheless, from the start he also willed that Pharaoh *not* let the Israelites go. In Exodus 4:21, God says to Moses: "When you go back to Egypt, see that you do before Pharaoh all the miracles that I have put in your power. But *I will harden his heart, so that he will not let the people go.*" At one point, Pharaoh himself acknowledges that his unwillingness to let the people go is sin: "Now therefore, forgive my sin" (Ex. 10:17). Thus, we see that God commanded that Pharaoh do a thing that God himself willed not to allow. The good thing that God commanded he prevented. And the thing he brought about involved sin.[6]

---

[4] "Characteristically John sees a fulfillment of Scripture in these happenings. The purpose of God had to be fulfilled. . . . Note the significance of the *hina* ['that']" (Leon Morris, *The Gospel According to John* [Grand Rapids: Eerdmans, 1971], 822).

[5] For a detailed study of the hardening texts in Exodus, see John Piper, *The Justification of God: An Exegetical and Theological Study of Romans 9:1–23* (Grand Rapids: Baker, 1993), 139–62. The relevant texts are Exodus 4:21; 7:3, 13, 14, 22; 8:15, 19, 32; 9:7, 12, 34, 35; 10:1, 20, 27; 11:10; 13:15; 14:4, 8, 17. Cf. G. K. Beale, "An Exegetical and Theological Consideration of the Hardening of Pharaoh's Heart in Exodus 4–14 and Romans 9," *Trinity Journal* 5 (1984), 129–54.

[6] This is illustrated also in the way the Lord worked so that the Egyptians hated his people, and then worked again so that the Israelites found favor with the Egyptians. Psalm 105:25: "[God] turned their

Some have tried to avoid this implication by pointing out that during the first five plagues the text does not say explicitly that God hardened Pharaoh's heart but that it "was hardened" (Ex. 7:22; 8:19; 9:7) or that Pharaoh hardened his own heart (Ex. 8:15, 32), and that only in the latter plagues does it say explicitly that God hardened Pharaoh's heart (Ex. 9:12; 10:20, 27; 11:10; 14:4). For example, R. T. Forster and V. P. Marston say that only from the sixth plague on did God give Pharaoh "supernatural strength to continue with his evil path of rebellion."[7]

But this observation does not succeed in avoiding the evidence of two wills in God. Even if Forster and Marston are right that God was not willing for Pharaoh's heart to be hardened during the first five plagues,[8] they concede that for the last five plagues God did will this, at least in the sense of strengthening Pharaoh to continue in the path of rebellion. Thus, there is a sense in which God did will that Pharaoh go on refusing to let the people go, and there is a sense in which he did will that Pharaoh release the people. For he commanded, "Let my people go." This illustrates why theologians talk about the "will of command" ("Let my people go!") and the "will of decree" ("God hardened Pharaoh's heart").

The exodus is not a unique instance of God's acting in this way. When the people of Israel reached the land of Sihon, king of Heshbon, Moses sent messengers "with words of peace, saying, 'Let me pass through your land. I will go only by the road'" (Deut. 2:26–27). Even though this request should have led Sihon to treat the people of God with respect, as God willed for his people to be blessed rather than attacked, nevertheless, "Sihon the king of

---

hearts to hate his people, to deal craftily with his servants." Exodus 12:36: "The LORD had given the people favor in the sight of the Egyptians, so that they let them have what they asked."

[7] R. T. Forster and V. P. Marston, *God's Strategy in Human History* (Wheaton, IL: Tyndale, 1973), 73.

[8] But they are probably wrong about this. The argument from the passive voice ("Pharaoh's heart *was hardened*"), that God is not the one hardening, will not work. The text implies that *God* is the one hardening even when the passive voice is used. We know this because the passive verb is followed by the phrase, "as the LORD had said," which refers back to Exodus 4:21 and 7:3, where God promises beforehand that he will harden Pharaoh's heart.

Heshbon would not let us pass by him, for *the LORD your God hardened his spirit and made his heart obstinate*, that he might give him into your hand, as he is this day" (v. 30). In other words, it was God's will (in one sense) that Sihon act in a way that was contrary to God's will (in another sense) that Israel be blessed and not cursed.

Similarly, the conquest of the cities of Canaan was owing to God's willing that the kings of the land resist Joshua rather than make peace with him. "Joshua made war a long time with all those kings. There was not a city that made peace with the people of Israel except the Hivites, the inhabitants of Gibeon. They took them all in battle. *For it was the LORD's doing to harden their hearts that they should come against Israel in battle, in order that they should be devoted to destruction* and should receive no mercy but be destroyed, just as the LORD commanded Moses" (Josh. 11:18–20).

In view of these examples, it is difficult to imagine what Fritz Guy means when he says that the "will of God" is always to be thought of in terms of loving desire and intention[9] rather than in terms of God's effective purpose of judgment. What seems more plain is that when the time has come for judgment, God wills that the guilty do things that are against his revealed will, such as cursing Israel rather than blessing her.

The hardening work of God is not limited to non-Israelites. In fact, it plays a central role in the life of Israel in the present period of history. In Romans 11:7–8, Paul speaks of Israel's failure to obtain the righteousness and salvation it desired: "Israel failed to obtain what it was seeking. The elect obtained it, but the rest were hardened, as it is written, 'God gave them a spirit of stupor, eyes that would not see and ears that would not hear, down to this very day.'" Even though it is the command of God that his people see, hear, and respond in faith (Isa. 42:18), nevertheless God has

---

[9] See note 12 in chapter 1.

his reasons for sending a spirit of stupor at times so that some will not obey his command.

Jesus expressed this same truth when he explained that one of his purposes in speaking in parables to the Jews of his day was to bring about this judicial blinding or stupor. In Mark 4:11–12 he says to his disciples, "To you has been given the secret of the kingdom of God, but for those outside everything is in parables, so that *'they may indeed see but not perceive, and may indeed hear but not understand*, lest they should turn and be forgiven.'" Here again God wills that a condition prevail that he regards as blameworthy. His will is that people turn and be forgiven (Mark 1:15), but he acts to restrict the fulfillment of that will.

Paul pictures this divine hardening as part of an overarching plan that will involve salvation for both Jew and Gentile. In Romans 11:25–26 he says to his Gentile readers: "Lest you be wise in your own sight, I do not want you to be unaware of this mystery, brothers: *a partial hardening has come upon Israel, until the fullness of the Gentiles has come in.* And in this way all Israel will be saved." The fact that the hardening has an appointed end—"until the fullness of the Gentiles has come in"—shows that it is part of God's plan rather than a merely contingent event outside God's purpose. Nevertheless, Paul expresses not only his but also God's heart when he says in Romans 10:1, "My heart's desire and prayer to God for them [Israel] is that they may be saved." God holds out his hands to a rebellious people (Rom. 10:21), but ordains a hardening that consigns them for a time to disobedience.

This is the point of Romans 11:31. Paul speaks to his Gentile readers again about the disobedience of Israel in rejecting their Messiah: "So they [Israel] too have now been disobedient *in order that* by the mercy shown to you [Gentiles] they also may now receive mercy." When Paul says that Israel was disobedient "in order that" the Gentiles might get the benefits of the gospel, whose purpose does he have in mind? It can only be God's. The people of

Israel did not conceive of their disobedience as a way of blessing the Gentiles or winning mercy for themselves in such a roundabout fashion. The point of Romans 11:31, therefore, is that God's hardening of Israel is not an end in itself, but is part of a saving purpose that will embrace all the nations. But in the short run, we have to say that God wills a condition (hardness of heart) that he commands people to strive against ("Do not harden your hearts," Heb. 3:8, 15; 4:7).

4. God's Right to Restrain Evil and His Will Not To

Another line of biblical evidence that God sometimes wills to bring about what he disapproves is his choosing to use or not to use his right to restrain evil in the human heart.

Proverbs 21:1 says, "The king's heart is a stream of water in the hand of the LORD; he turns it wherever he will." An illustration of this divine right over the king's heart is given in Genesis 20. Abraham is sojourning in Gerar and tells King Abimelech that Sarah is his sister. So Abimelech takes her as part of his harem. But God is displeased and warns Abimelech in a dream that she is married to Abraham. Abimelech protests to God that he took her in his integrity. And God says, "Yes, I know that you have done this in the integrity of your heart, and *it was I who kept you from sinning against me. Therefore I did not let you touch her*" (v. 6).

What is apparent here is that God has the right and the power to restrain the sins of secular rulers. When he does, it is his will to do it. And when he does not, it is his will not to. That is to say, sometimes God wills that their sins be restrained and sometimes he wills that they increase more than if he restrained them.[10]

It is not an unjust infringement on human agency that the Creator has the right and power to restrain the evil actions of his creatures. Psalm 33:10–11 says: "The LORD brings the counsel of

---

[10] Examples of God stirring up the hearts of kings to do his will include 1 Chronicles 5:25–26 (cf. 2 Kings 15:19) and 2 Chronicles 36:22–23 (cf. Ezra 1:1–3).

the nations to nothing; he frustrates the plans of the peoples. The counsel of the LORD stands forever, the plans of his heart to all generations." Sometimes God frustrates the will of rulers by making their plans fail. Sometimes he does so by influencing their hearts the way he did with Abimelech, without their even knowing it.

But there are times when God does not use this right because he intends for human evil to run its course. For example, God meant to put the sons of Eli to death. Therefore, he willed that they not listen to their father's counsel:

> Now Eli was very old, and he kept hearing all that his sons were doing to all Israel, and how they lay with the women who were serving at the entrance to the tent of meeting. And he said to them, "Why do you do such things? For I hear of your evil dealings from all these people. No, my sons; it is no good report that I hear the people of the LORD spreading abroad. If someone sins against a man, God will mediate for him, but if someone sins against the LORD, who can intercede for him?" But they would not listen to the voice of their father, for it was the will of the LORD to put them to death. (1 Sam. 2:22–25)

Why would the sons of Eli not heed their father's good counsel? The answer of the text is "*for* it was the will of the LORD to put them to death." This makes sense only if the Lord had the right and the power to restrain their disobedience—a right and power that he willed not to use. Thus, we must say that in one sense God willed that the sons of Eli go on doing what he commanded them not to do: dishonoring their father and committing sexual immorality.

Moreover, the word translated as "will" in the clause "it was the *will* of the LORD to put them to death" is the same Hebrew word (*haphez*) used in Ezekiel 18:23, 32 and 33:11, where God asserts that he does not *have pleasure* in the death of the wicked. The word signifies desire or pleasure. God (in one sense) *desired* to put the sons of Eli to death, but (in another sense) he does not *desire* the death of the wicked. This is a strong warning to us not to take one assertion, such as Ezekiel 18:23, and assume we know the precise meaning without letting other passages, such as 1 Samuel 2:25, have a say. The upshot of putting the two together is that in one sense God may desire the death of the wicked and in another sense he may not.

Another illustration of God's choosing not to use his right to restrain evil is found in Romans 1:24–28. Three times Paul says that God *gave people up* to sink further into corruption. Verse 24: "Therefore God gave them up in the lusts of their hearts to impurity." Verse 26: "For this reason God gave them up to dishonorable passions." Verse 28: "And since they did not see fit to acknowledge God, God gave them up to a debased mind."

God had the right and the power to restrain this evil the way he did for Abimelech. But he did not will to do that. Rather, his will in this case was to punish, and part of God's punishment of evil is sometimes willing that the evil increase. But this means that God chooses for behavior to come about that he commands not to happen. The fact that God's willing is punitive does not change that. And the fact that it is *justifiably* punitive is one of the points of this book. There are other examples we could give,[11] but we pass on to a different line of evidence.

---

[11] Other examples of God's not restraining evil because he planned to use it include:

1. "The Lord had ordained to defeat the good counsel of Ahithophel, so that the Lord might bring harm upon Absalom" (2 Sam. 17:14).

2. When Rehoboam, the son of Solomon, was considering how to rule the people, he took into consideration the will of the people that he lighten the yoke that Solomon had put on them (1 Kings 12:9). He also consulted with the young and with the old men. He decided to follow the counsel of the young, who said he should make the yoke harder. Why did this come about? First Kings 12:15 gives the answer: "So the king did not listen to the people, for *it was a turn of affairs brought about by the Lord that he might fulfill his word*, which the Lord spoke by Ahijah the Shilonite to Jeroboam the son of Nebat." This is important to show again (as with Rev. 17:17) that the fulfillment of prophecy (1 Kings 11:29–39) is by a work of the Lord: "It was a turn of affairs brought about by the Lord." Prophecy is not mere foreknowledge of what will come about somehow on its own. Prophecy is an expression of what God intends to bring about in the future.

3. To his father's dismay, Samson insisted that his father take a wife for him from the Philistines. His father counseled against it, just as Eli tried to restrain the evil of his sons. But Samson prevailed.

5. Does God Delight in the Punishment of the Wicked?

We just saw that it was God's "will" (or "desire") to put the sons of Eli to death, and that the word translated as "will" is the same one used in Ezekiel 18:23 when God says he does not *have pleasure* in the death of the wicked. Another illustration of this complex willing (or desiring, or having pleasure) is found in Deuteronomy 28:63. Moses warns about coming judgment on unrepentant Israel. What he says is strikingly different (not contradictory, I will argue) from Ezekiel 18:23. "And as the LORD took delight in doing you good and multiplying you, so the LORD will take delight in bringing ruin upon you and destroying you" (v. 63). Here, an even stronger word (*yasis*) for pleasure is used when the text says that God will "take delight in bringing ruin upon you and destroying you."

We are faced with the inescapable biblical fact that in some sense God does not delight in the death of the wicked (Ezekiel 18) and in some sense he does (Deut. 28:63; 1 Sam. 2:25).[12] As we move toward a resolution of this apparent contradiction, let us turn now to ponder the extent of God's sovereignty that lies behind it.

Why? "His father and mother did not know that *it was from the* LORD, for he was seeking an opportunity against the Philistines" (Judg. 14:4).

4. In Deuteronomy 29:2–4, Moses explains why the people have not been more responsive to God and why they have gone their own way so often: "You have seen all that the LORD did before your eyes in the land of Egypt . . . the signs, and those great wonders. But to this day *the* LORD *has not given you a heart to understand or eyes to see or ears to hear*."

[12] One should also take heed to the texts that portray God laughing over the ruin of the defiant (Prov. 1:24–26; Rev. 18:20).

3

How Extensive Is the Sovereign Will of God?

Behind the complex relationship of the two wills in God is the foundational biblical premise that God is sovereign in a way that makes him ruler of all actions. R. T. Forster and V. P. Marston try to overcome the tension between God's will of decree and God's will of command by asserting that there is no such thing as his sovereign will of decree: "Nothing in Scripture suggests that there is some kind of will or plan of God which is inviolable."[1] This is a remarkable claim. Without making an exhaustive survey, it will be fair to touch on some Scripture passages that do indeed suggest "that there is some kind of will or plan of God which is inviolable."

Sovereign over Calamities

There are passages that ascribe to God the final control over all calamities and disasters wrought by nature or by man. Amos 3:6:

---

[1] R. T. Forster and V. P. Marston, *God's Strategy in Human History* (Wheaton, IL: Tyndale, 1973), 32. Their favorite text to demonstrate that God's will for people is contingent and not effectual is Luke 7:30: "The Pharisees and the lawyers rejected the purpose of God for themselves, not having been baptized by him" (RSV). However, the phrase "for themselves," because of its location in the word order, very likely does not modify "the purpose of God" (as the RSV might suggest). Rather, it probably modifies "rejected." Thus, Luke is saying that the plan of salvation preached by John the Baptist was accepted by some and rejected by others "for themselves." The text cannot prove one way or the other whether God has a specific plan for each life that can be successfully frustrated.

"Does disaster come to a city, unless the LORD has done it?"; Isaiah 45:6–7: "I am the LORD, and there is no other. I form light and create darkness, I make well-being and create calamity, I am the LORD, who does all these things"; Lamentations 3:37–38: "Who has spoken and it came to pass, unless the Lord has commanded it? Is it not from the mouth of the Most High that good and bad come?" Noteworthy in these texts is that the calamities in view involve human hostilities and cruelties that God disapproves even as he wills that they occur.

Peter's Two Ways of Seeing God's Will

The apostle Peter wrote concerning God's involvement in the sufferings of his people at the hands of their antagonists. In his first letter, he speaks of the "will of God" in two senses. On one hand, it is something to be pursued and lived up to: "This is *the will of God*, that by doing good you should put to silence the ignorance of foolish people" (1 Pet. 2:15). "Live for the rest of the time in the flesh no longer for human passions but for *the will of God*" (4:2).

On the other hand, the will of God is not his moral instruction, but the state of affairs that he sovereignly brings about. "For it is better to suffer for doing good, *if that should be God's will*, than for doing evil" (3:17). "Let those who suffer *according to God's will* entrust their souls to a faithful Creator while doing good" (4:19). In this context, the suffering that Peter has in mind is that which comes from hostile people and therefore cannot come without sin.

"If the Lord Wills"

In fact, the New Testament saints seemed to live in the calm light of an overarching sovereignty of God concerning all the details of their lives and ministries. Paul expresses himself like this with regard to his travel plans. On taking leave of the saints in Ephesus, he says, "I will return to you *if God wills*" (Acts 18:21). To the Corinthians he writes, "I will come to you soon, *if the Lord wills*" (1 Cor. 4:19). And again, "I do not want to see you now just in passing. I hope to spend some time with you, *if the Lord permits*" (16:7).

The writer to the Hebrews says that he intends to leave elementary things behind and press on to maturity. But then he pauses and adds, "And this we will do *if God permits*" (Heb. 6:3). This is remarkable, since it is hard to imagine one even thinking that God might not permit such a thing unless one has a remarkably high view of the sovereign prerogatives of God.

James warns against the pride of presumption in speaking of the simplest plans in life without a due submission to the overarching sovereignty of God over the day's agenda. Man's plans might be interrupted by God's decision to take the life he gave. Instead of saying, "'Today or tomorrow we will go into such and such a town and spend a year there and trade and make a profit' . . . you ought to say, '*If the Lord wills*, we will live and do this or that'" (James 4:13–15).[2] Thus, the saints in Caesarea, when they could not dissuade Paul from taking the risk to go to Jerusalem, "ceased and said, '*Let the will of the Lord* be done'" (Acts 21:14). God would decide whether Paul would be killed or not, just as James said.

It Is an Old Teaching

This sense of living in the hands of God, right down to the details of life, was not new for the early Christians. They knew of it from the whole history of Israel, but especially from their Wisdom Lit-

---

[2] Randall G. Basinger argues that belief in the absolute sovereignty of God is practically irrelevant in daily life. Of all the things that could be said against this view, the most important one seems to be that James, writing under the inspiration of God, does not share it, but teaches that a life lived without a conscious submission to the sovereignty of God in everyday affairs is tantamount to boasting in arrogance (James 4:16) (Randall G. Basinger, "Exhaustive Divine Sovereignty: A Practical Critique," in *A Case for Arminianism: The Grace of God, the Will of Man*, gen. ed. Clark H. Pinnock [Grand Rapids: Zondervan, 1989]. See also Jerry Bridges, "Does Divine Sovereignty Make a Difference in Everyday Life?" in *Still Sovereign: Contemporary Perspectives on Election, Foreknowledge, and Grace*, eds. Thomas R. Schreiner and Bruce A. Ware [Grand Rapids: Baker, 2000], 295–306).

erature. "The plans of the heart belong to man, but the answer of the tongue is from the LORD" (Prov. 16:1). "The heart of man plans his way, but the LORD establishes his steps" (v. 9). "The lot is cast into the lap, but its every decision is from the LORD" (v. 33). "Many are the plans in the mind of a man, but it is the purpose of the LORD that will stand" (19:21). "I know, O LORD, that the way of man is not in himself, that it is not in man who walks to direct his steps" (Jer. 10:23). Jesus had no quarrel with this sense of living in the hand of God. If anything, he intensified the idea with words such as these: "Are not two sparrows sold for a penny? And not one of them will fall to the ground apart from your Father" (Matt. 10:29).

So the Prophets Saw the World

This confidence that the details of life are in the control of God every day was rooted in numerous prophetic expressions of God's unstoppable, unthwartable sovereign purpose. "Remember the former things of old; for I am God, and there is no other; I am God, and there is none like me, declaring the end from the beginning and from ancient times things not yet done, saying, '*My counsel shall stand, and I will accomplish all my purpose*'" (Isa. 46:9–10; cf. 43:13). "All the inhabitants of the earth are accounted as nothing, and *he does according to his will among the host of heaven and among the inhabitants of the earth; and none can stay his hand or say to him, 'What have you done?*'" (Dan. 4:35). "I know that you can do all things, and that *no purpose of yours can be thwarted*" (Job 42:2). "Our God is in the heavens; he does all that he pleases" (Ps. 115:3).

The Preciousness of New Covenant Sovereignty

One of the most precious implications of this confidence in God's inviolable sovereign will is that it provides the foundation of the "new covenant" hope for the holiness without which we will not see the Lord (Heb. 12:14). In the old covenant, the law was written on stone and brought death when it met with the resistance of unrenewed hearts. But the new covenant promise is that God will not let his purposes for a holy people shipwreck on the weakness of human will. Instead, he promises to do what needs to be done to make us what we ought to be. "And the LORD your God will circumcise your heart and the heart of your offspring, so that you will love the LORD your God with all your heart and with all your soul, that you may live" (Deut. 30:6). "I will put my Spirit within you, and cause you to walk in my statutes and be careful to obey my rules" (Ezek. 36:27). "I will make with them an everlasting covenant, that I will not turn away from doing good to them. And I will put the fear of me in their hearts, that they may not turn from me" (Jer. 32:40). "Work out your own salvation with fear and trembling, *for it is God who works in you, both to will and to work for his good pleasure*" (Phil. 2:12–13).

God's Will as Moral Standards and Sovereign Control

In view of all these texts, I am unable to grasp what Forster and Marston might mean by saying, "Nothing in Scripture suggests that there is some kind of will or plan of God which is inviolable" (see note 1). Neither can I understand how Fritz Guy can say that the "will of God" is always a desiring and an intending but not a sovereign, effective willing (see note 12, chapter 1). Rather, the Scriptures lead us again and again to affirm that God's will is sometimes spoken of as an expression of his moral standards for human behavior and sometimes as an expression of his sovereign control even over acts that are contrary to that standard.

This means that the distinction between terms such as "will of decree" and "will of command," or "sovereign will" and "moral will," is not an artificial distinction demanded by Reformed theology. The terms are an effort to describe the whole of biblical revelation. They are an effort to say yes to all of the Bible and not silence any of it. They are a way to say yes to the universal, saving will of Ezekiel 18:23 and Matthew 23:37, and yes to the individual, unconditional election of Romans 9:6–23.[3]

---

[3] That Romans 9:23 does in fact deal with individuals and eternal destinies, and not just with groups and historical roles, is the thesis of John Piper, *The Justification of God: An Exegetical and Theological Study of Romans 9:1–23* (Grand Rapids: Baker, 1993), and to my knowledge the arguments presented there have not been gainsaid. From the one passing reference to this study by Pinnock in *A Case for Arminianism*, it seems that serious attention has not been paid to the arguments I gave there. Pinnock has a legitimate concern that Romans 9 be interpreted with Romans 10 and 11 in view. He says: "I believe that if Piper had moved forward in Romans beyond Romans 9, he would have encountered Paul's earnest prayer to God that the lost be saved (10:1) and his explanation of how it happens that any are actually included or excluded—through faith or the lack of it (11:20). Romans 9 must be read in the context of the larger context of Romans 9–11" (Pinnock, "From Augustine to Arminius: A Pilgrimage in Theology," in *A Case for Arminianism*, 29, note 10). I certainly do not disagree that Romans 9 must be read in its context. That is why, for example, on pages 9–15 and 163–5 of *The Justification of God*, I discussed the limits of my focus on Romans 9:1–23 within the structure of Romans 9–11. With regard to Pinnock's two specific points: it is true that we are included or excluded in salvation on the condition of faith. But that does not account for how one person comes to faith and not another. Neither does Paul's "heart's desire and prayer to God" for the salvation of the Jews in Romans 10:1 contradict the explicit statement that "a partial hardening has come [from God] upon Israel, until [God lifts it after] the fullness of the Gentiles [appointed by God for salvation] has come in" (Rom. 11:25). See also Thomas R. Schreiner, "Does Romans 9 Teach Individual Election Unto Salvation?" in *Still Sovereign*, 89–106.

4

Does It Make Sense?

I turn now to the task of reflecting on how these two wills of God fit together and make sense—as far as a finite and fallible creature can rise to that challenge.

God Does Not Sin in Willing That Sin Takes Place

The first thing to affirm in view of all these texts is that God does not sin. "Holy, holy, holy is the LORD of hosts; the whole earth is full of his glory" (Isa. 6:3). "God cannot be tempted with evil, and he himself tempts no one" (James 1:13).[1] In ordering all things, in-

---

[1] I am aware that James 1:13–14 is a text some would use against my position: "Let no one say when he is tempted, 'I am being tempted by God,' for God cannot be tempted with evil, and he himself tempts no one. But each person is tempted when he is lured and enticed by his own desire." There is no point in hiding each other's problem texts. I am not allowed to pick and choose any more than others may neglect all the texts I have cited. If I cannot make texts harmonize, I try to let them both stand until someone wiser than I can (even if I must wait for God's final enlightenment in heaven). My effort at understanding James 1:13, in view of all the examples of God's purpose that sinful actions come about, is to say that God "tempt" is defined in verse 14 as being "lured" (*exelkomenos*) and "enticed" (*deleazomenos*). In other words, James is not thinking of temptation in terms of an object of desire being put in front of someone (e.g., he does not attribute "temptation" to Satan, the arch "tempter," but to our "desire"). For example, temptation is not the pornography on display, in James's way of thinking here; rather, it is the "luring" and "enticing" of the soul that makes a person want to look. He is thinking of temptation as the engagement of the emotions in strong desires for evil. This he calls the "conceiving" (*syllabousa*) stage of temptation before the actual "birth" (*tiktei*) of the act of sin (James 1:15). Thus, it seems to me that James is saying that God does not ever have this experience of being "lured" or "enticed." And he does not directly (see note 7 below) produce that "luring" and "enticing" toward evil in humans. In some way (that we may not be able to fully comprehend), God is able without blameworthy "tempting" to see to it that a person does what he ordains for him to do, even if it involves evil.

But James is not saying that God cannot have objective enticements to evil put in front of him or that he himself does not arrange events at times so that such enticements come before us, which

cluding sinful acts, God is not sinning. As Jonathan Edwards says: "It implies no contradiction to suppose that an act may be an evil act, and yet that it is a good thing that such an act should come to pass. . . . As for instance, it might be an evil thing to crucify Christ, but yet it was a good thing that the crucifying of Christ came to pass."[2] In other words, the Scriptures lead us to the insight that God can will that a sinful act come to pass without willing it as an act of sin in himself.

Edwards points out that Arminians, it seems, must come to a similar conclusion:

> All must own that God sometimes wills not to hinder the breach of his own commands, because he does not in fact hinder it. . . . But you will say, God wills to permit sin, as he wills the creature should be left to his freedom; and if he should hinder it, he would offer violence to the nature of his own creature. I answer, this comes nevertheless to the very same thing that I say. You say, God does not will sin absolutely; but, rather than alter the law of nature and the nature of free agents, he wills it. He wills what is contrary to excellency in some particulars, for the sake of a more general excellency and order. So that the scheme of the Arminians does not help the matter.[3]

What Keeps God from Saving Whom He Desires to Save?

This seems right to me, and it can be illustrated again by reflecting directly on 1 Timothy 2:4, where Paul says that God "desires all people to be saved and to come to the knowledge of the truth." What are we to say of the fact that God desires something that

---

may lead us, through the "luring" of our desires, to sin (which God knew would happen and, in one sense, willed). In fact, the Bible reveals that God tests (the same word as "tempt" in Greek) his people often (cf. Heb. 11:17) by arranging their circumstances so that they are presented with dangerous acts of obedience that they might sinfully fear, or sinful pleasures that they might covet. In the end, I say that God is able to order events, if it seems wise and good to do so, such that sin comes about; yet he does so without "tempting" those who sin, as James says.

[2] Jonathan Edwards, "Concerning the Decrees in General, and Election in Particular," in *The Works of Jonathan Edwards*, vol. 2 (Edinburgh: The Banner of Truth Trust, 1974), 529.

[3] Ibid., 528.

in fact does not happen? There are two possibilities, as far as I can see.

One possibility is that there is a power in the universe greater than God's, which is frustrating him by overruling what he desires. Neither the Reformed nor the Arminians affirm this. The other possibility is that God wills not to save all, even though he "desires" that all be saved, because there is something else that he wills or desires more, which would be lost if he exerted his sovereign power to save all. This is the solution that I, as Reformed, affirm along with Arminians. In other words, both the Reformed and the Arminians affirm two wills in God when they ponder deeply over 1 Timothy 2:4 (as we have seen in the case of I. Howard Marshall). Both can say that God wills for all to be saved. And when queried *why* all are not saved, both the Reformed and the Arminians answer the same: because God is committed to something even more valuable than saving all.

The difference between the Reformed and the Arminians lies not in whether there are two wills in God, but in what they say this higher commitment is. What does God will more than saving all? The answer the Arminians give is that human self-determination and the possible resulting love relationship with God are more valuable than saving all people by sovereign, efficacious grace. The answer the Reformed give is that the greater value is the manifestation of the full range of God's glory in wrath and mercy (Rom. 9:22–23) and the humbling of man so that he enjoys giving all credit to God for his salvation (1 Cor. 1:29).

This Controversial Text Does Not Settle the Matter

This is utterly crucial to see, for it implies that 1 Timothy 2:4 does not settle the momentous issue of God's higher commitment that restrains him from saving all. There is no mention here of human free will that might thwart God's will.[4] Neither is there mention

---

[4] In fact, 2 Timothy 2:24–26 teaches that self-determination is not the decisive factor in repenting and coming to a knowledge of the truth (see note 14, chapter 1): "And the Lord's servant must not

of God's sovereign, prevenient, efficacious grace as the force that might determine that some are saved and some not. The text is silent about both of these possible explanations as to why not all are saved. If all we had was this text, we could only guess what restrains God from saving all. When some people say there is human free will in 1 Timothy 2:4, that is owing to a philosophical presupposition, not an exegetical conclusion.

What Is Free Will?

Before I mention what that presupposition is, let me make sure we have a clear definition of what I mean by "free will." The definition of free will that I think is most helpful in theological debates is "ultimate (or decisive) human self-determination." By "ultimate" or "decisive," I mean that, whatever other influences may lead toward a decision, the influence that settles the choice is the human self. Most Arminians and Open Theists[5] accept this definition as long as I make clear that the self-determination is a gift of God. As one Open Theist has said: "Once God gives the gift of self-determination, he *has to*, within limits, endure its misuse. . . . The *genuineness* of the gift of self-determination hinges on its *irrevocability*."[6]

Reading a Philosophical Presupposition into 1 Timothy 2:4

I said above that some people read into 1 Timothy 2:4 (God "desires all people to be saved and to come to the knowledge of the

---

be quarrelsome but kind to everyone, able to teach, patiently enduring evil, correcting his opponents with gentleness. *God may perhaps grant them repentance* leading to a knowledge of the truth, and they may come to their senses and escape from the snare of the devil, after being captured by him to do his will."

[5] Open Theists push the logic of Arminianism further than historic Arminians have been willing to go. They argue that for human will to be truly free, it cannot be certainly foreknown, even by God, for if God foreknows something certainly, it must necessarily come to pass. But if an act is necessary, it cannot be free. Therefore, Open Theists deny the exhaustive foreknowledge of God. See Greg Boyd, *God of the Possible: A Biblical Introduction to the Open View of God* (Grand Rapids: Baker, 2000).

[6] Greg Boyd, *Satan and the Problem of Evil: Constructing a Trinitarian Warfare Theodicy* (Downers Grove, IL: InterVarsity Press, 2001), 181–2.

truth") the necessity of free will as an explanation for why all are not saved. I said this is not owing to anything in the text, but to a philosophical presupposition brought to the text. The presupposition is that, if God wills in one sense for all to be saved, then he cannot will in another sense that only some be saved.

In fact, the wider context of the Pastoral Epistles points away from free will as a solution. Paul uses the very language of 1 Timothy 2:4 again in 2 Timothy 2:24–26: "And the Lord's servant must not be quarrelsome but kind to everyone, able to teach, patiently enduring evil, correcting his opponents with gentleness. *God may perhaps grant them repentance* leading to *a knowledge of the truth*, and they may come to their senses and escape from the snare of the devil, after being captured by him to do his will." I tried to show earlier (see note 14, chapter 1) that Paul here is explaining why some do not "come to the knowledge of the truth." The ultimate or decisive answer is that God himself may or may not "grant . . . repentance leading to a knowledge of the truth."

Therefore, the presupposition that seems to demand free will as an explanation for why not all are saved in spite of 1 Timothy 2:4 is not in the text, is not demanded by logic, is not in harmony with the wider context of the Pastoral Epistles, and is not taught in the rest of Scripture. Therefore, 1 Timothy 2:4 does not settle the issue. Both Reformed and Arminian thinkers must look elsewhere to answer whether the preservation of ultimate human self-determination (free will) or the manifestation of the glory of divine sovereignty is what restrains God's will to save all people.

The Best Thinkers Do Not Oversimplify

The Reformed thinkers whom I admire most do not claim to have simple, easy solutions to complex biblical tensions. When their writing is difficult, this is because the Scriptures are difficult (as the apostle Peter admitted that they sometimes are, 2 Pet. 3:16). These Reformed pastors and theologians are struggling to be faithful to diverse (but not contradictory) Scripture passages. Both the Reformed and the Arminians feel at times that the ridicule directed against their complex expositions is, in fact, a ridicule against the complexity of the Scriptures.

For example, I find the effort of Stephen Charnock (1628–1680), a chaplain to Henry Cromwell and a Nonconformist pastor in London, to be balanced and helpful in holding the diverse Scripture passages on God's will together. Before I quote him, consider with me something that he touches on with regard to God's forbidding people to do evil and yet willing that evil take place. Charnock deals with the notion of God's willing things *directly* or not. That is, God sometimes wills for evil to happen by means of secondary causes.

Is It Biblical to Think of Secondary Causes?

Arminians sometimes disparage Reformed appeals to "secondary causes" between God's sovereign will and the immediate effecting of a sinful act.[7] But the Reformed introduce this idea of intermediate causes, different from God's ultimate causing, not because of a theological necessity but because so many Scripture passages demand it. For example, God commissions an "evil spirit" between Abimelech and the men of Shechem to bring about his will (Judg. 9:22–24); Satan leads Judas to do (Luke 22:3) what Acts 2:23 says God brings about; Paul says that Satan blinds the minds of unbelievers (2 Cor. 4:4), but also says that God sends a blinding spirit of stupor (Rom. 11:8–10); Satan stirs up David to take a census (1 Chron. 21:1), which proves to be sin (2 Sam. 24:10), and yet it is written that God is in some sense the cause behind Satan (2 Sam. 24:1); and Satan gets permission from God to torment Job (Job 1:12; 2:6), but when Satan takes Job's family and makes him sick,

---

[7] For example, Jack Cottrell, "The Nature of Divine Sovereignty," in Clark H. Pinnock, gen. ed., *A Case for Arminianism: The Grace of God, the Will of Man* (Grand Rapids: Zondervan, 1989), 100–102.

Job says, "The LORD has taken" (Job 1:21), and, "Shall we receive good from God, and shall we not receive evil?" (2:10)—to which the writer responds: "In all this Job did not sin or charge God with wrong" (1:22; cf. 2:10).

Texts such as these make the theological reflections of Theodore Beza (in 1582) biblically sound:

> Nothing happens . . . without God's most righteous decree, although God is not the author of or sharer in any sin at all. Both His power and His goodness are so great and so incomprehensible, that at a time when He applies the devil or wicked men in achieving some work, whom He afterwards justly punishes, He Himself nonetheless effects His holy work well and justly. These things do not hinder but rather establish second and intermediate causes, by which all things happen. When from eternity God decreed whatever was to happen at definite moments, He at the same time also decreed the manner and way which He wished it thus to take place; to such extent, that even if some flaw is discovered in a second cause, it yet implies no flaw or fault in God's eternal counsel.[8]

Stephen Charnock and Jonathan Edwards

Now back to my point that rigorously biblical Reformed and Arminian thinkers realize that sometimes the complexity of our theological solutions is owing to the complexity of the biblical text. Therefore, I have a high level of respect for efforts such as those of Charnock and Edwards to help us hold together the diverse passages on God's will. Charnock writes:

> God doth not will [sin] directly, and by an efficacious will. He doth not directly will it, because he hath prohibited it by his law, which is a discovery of his will; so that if he should directly will sin, and directly prohibit it, he would will good and evil in the

---

[8] Theodore Beza, cited in Heinrich Heppe, *Reformed Dogmatics* (1860; repr., Grand Rapids: Baker, 1978), 143–4.

same manner, and there would be contradictions in God's will: to will sin absolutely, is to work it (Psalm 115:3): "God hath done whatsoever he pleased." God cannot absolutely will it, because he cannot work it. God wills good by a positive decree, because he hath decreed to effect it. He wills evil by a private decree, because he hath decreed not to give that grace which would certainly prevent it. God doth not will sin simply, for that were to approve it, but he wills it, in order to that good his wisdom will bring forth from it. He wills not sin for itself, but for the event.[9]

Edwards, writing about eighty years later, comes to similar conclusions using somewhat different terminology.

When a distinction is made between God's revealed will and his secret will, or his will of command and decree, "will" is certainly in that distinction taken in two senses. His will of decree, is not his will in the same sense as his will of command is. Therefore, it is no difficulty at all to suppose, that the one may be otherwise than the other: his will in both senses is his inclination. But when we say he wills virtue, or loves virtue, or the happiness of his creature; thereby is intended, that virtue, or the creature's happiness, absolutely and simply considered, is agreeable to the inclination of his nature.

His will of decree is, his inclination to a thing, not as to that thing absolutely and simply, but with respect to the universality of things, that have been, are, or shall be. So God, though he hates a thing as it is simply, may incline to it with reference to the universality of things. Though he hates sin in itself, yet he may will to permit it, for the greater promotion of holiness in this universality, including all things, and at all times. So, though he has no inclination to a creature's misery, considered absolutely, yet he may will it, for the greater promotion of happiness in this universality.[10]

---

[9] Stephen Charnock, *Discourses upon the Existence and Attributes of God* (Grand Rapids: Baker, 1979), 148.
[10] Edwards, "Concerning the Decrees," 527–8.

God Sees the World through Two Lenses

Putting it in my own words, Edwards says that the infinite complexity of the divine mind is such that God has the capacity to look at the world through two lenses. He can look through a narrow lens or through a wide-angle lens. When God looks at a painful or wicked event through his narrow lens, he sees the tragedy or the sin for what it is in itself, and he is angered and grieved. "I have no pleasure in the death of anyone, declares the Lord GOD" (Ezek. 18:32). "Let no corrupting talk come out of your mouths. . . . And do not grieve the Holy Spirit of God" (Eph. 4:29–30).

But when God looks at a painful or wicked event through his wide-angle lens, he sees the tragedy or the sin in relation to everything leading up to it and everything flowing out from it. He sees it in all the connections and effects that form a pattern or mosaic stretching into eternity. This mosaic, with all its (good and evil) parts, he does delight in (Ps. 115:3). Or, again, as Edwards says, "God, though he hates a thing as it is simply, may incline to it with reference to the universality of things."

The Incomprehensible Complexity of God's Emotional Life

God's emotional life is infinitely complex beyond our ability to fully comprehend. For example, who can comprehend that the Lord hears in one moment of time the prayers of millions of Christians around the world, and sympathizes with each one personally and individually (as Heb. 4:15 says), even though among those millions of praying Christians some are broken-hearted and some are bursting with joy? How can God "weep with those who weep" and "rejoice with those who rejoice" (Rom. 12:15) when both are coming to him at the same time—in fact, are always coming to him, with no break at all?

Or who can comprehend that God is angry at the sin of the world every day (Ps. 7:11), and yet every day, every moment, he is rejoicing with tremendous joy because somewhere in the world a sinner is repenting (Luke 15:7, 10, 23)? Who can comprehend that God grieves over the unholy speech of his people (Eph. 4:29–30), yet takes pleasure in them daily (Ps. 149:4)?

Who of us could say what complex of emotions is not possible for God? All we have to go on here is what he has chosen to tell us in the Bible. And what he has told us is that there is a sense in which he does not experience pleasure in the judgment of the wicked, and there is a sense in which he does. There is a sense in which he desires that all be saved and a sense in which he does not.

God's Wisdom Is His Highest Counselor

Therefore, we should not stumble over the fact that God does and does not take pleasure in the death of the wicked. When Moses warns Israel that the Lord will take delight in bringing ruin upon them and destroying them if they do not repent (Deut. 28:63), he means that those who have rebelled against the Lord and moved beyond repentance will not be able to gloat that they have made the Almighty miserable. God is not defeated in the triumphs of his righteous judgment. Quite the contrary. Moses tells the people that when they are judged, they will unwittingly provide an occasion for God to rejoice in the demonstration of his justice. This is Paul's answer as well. In the demonstration of his wrath, he displays his power and the infinite worth of his glory (Rom. 9:22–23)—which is what he wills to do.[11]

When God took counsel with himself as to whether he should save all people, he consulted not only the truth of what he sees when looking through the narrow lens, but also the larger truth of what he sees through the wide-angle lens of his all-knowing wis-

---

[11] This is the way Edwards tackled the problem of how God and the saints will be happy in heaven for all eternity, even though they will know that many millions of people are suffering in hell forever. It is not that suffering or misery in itself will be pleasant to God and to the saints, but that the vindication of God's infinite holiness will be cherished so deeply. See John Gerstner, *Jonathan Edwards on Heaven and Hell* (Grand Rapids: Baker, 1980), 33–38.

dom. The result of this consultation with his own infinite wisdom was that God deemed it wise and good to elect unconditionally some to salvation and not others. This raises another form of the question we have been wrestling with. Is the free offer of salvation to everyone genuine? Is it made with a sincere heart? Does it come from real compassion? Is the willing that none perish a bona fide willing of love?

George Washington and the Sincerity of God's Saving Will

The way I would give an account of this is explained by Robert L. Dabney in an essay written more than one hundred years ago.[12] His treatment is very detailed and answers many objections that go beyond the limits of this book. I will simply give the essence of his solution, which seems to me to be on the right track, though he, as well as I, would admit we do not "furnish an exhaustive explanation of this mystery of the divine will."[13]

Dabney uses an analogy from the life of George Washington, taken from Chief Justice John Marshall's *Life of Washington*. A Major John André had jeopardized the safety of the young United States of America through "rash and unfortunate" treasonous acts, and Washington faced a decision on the major's punishment. Marshall says of Washington's signing of the death warrant for André, "Perhaps on no occasion of his life did the commander-in-chief obey with more reluctance the stern mandates of duty and of policy." Dabney observes that Washington's compassion for André was "real and profound." He also had "plenary power to kill or to save alive." Why, then, did he sign the death warrant? Dabney explains, "Washington's volition to sign the death-warrant of André

---

[12] Robert L. Dabney, "God's Indiscriminate Proposals of Mercy, as Related to His Power, Wisdom, and Sincerity," in *Discussions: Evangelical and Theological*, vol. 1 (1890; repr., Edinburgh: The Banner of Truth Trust, 1967), 282–313. This treatment of Dabney has been published previously in John Piper, *The Pleasures of God: Meditations on God's Delight in Being God*, third edition (Colorado Springs: Multnomah, 2012), 145–6.
[13] Dabney, "God's Indiscriminate Proposals of Mercy," 309.

did not arise from the fact that his compassion was slight or feigned [the narrow lens], but from the fact that it was rationally counterpoised by a complex of superior judgments . . . of wisdom, duty, patriotism, and moral indignation [the wide-angle lens]."

Dabney imagines a defender of André hearing Washington say, "I do this with the deepest reluctance and pity." Then the defender says, "Since you are supreme in this matter, and have full bodily ability to throw down that pen, we shall know by your signing this warrant that your pity is hypocritical." Dabney responds to this by saying: "The petulance of this charge would have been equal to its folly. The pity was real, but was restrained by superior elements of motive. Washington had official and bodily power to discharge the criminal, but he had not the sanctions of his own wisdom and justice."[14] The corresponding point in the case of divine election is that "the absence of [effective] volition in God to save does not necessarily imply the absence of compassion."[15] God has "a true compassion, which is yet restrained, in the case of the . . . non-elect, by consistent and holy reasons, from taking the form of a volition to regenerate."[16] God's infinite wisdom "regulates his whole will and guides and harmonizes (not suppresses) all its active principles."[17]

What God Does Not Will "from His Heart"

In other words, God has a real and deep compassion for perishing sinners. Jeremiah points to this reality in God's heart. In Lamentations 3:32–33, he speaks of the judgment that God has brought upon Jerusalem: "Though he cause grief, he will have compassion according to the abundance of his steadfast love; for he does not afflict *from his heart* or grieve the children of men." It appears that this is Jeremiah's way of saying that God *does* will the affliction that he causes, but he does *not* will it in the same way he wills com-

---

14 Ibid., 285.
15 Ibid., 299.
16 Ibid., 307.
17 Ibid., 309.

passion. The affliction does not come "from his heart." Jeremiah was trying, as we are, to come to terms with the way a sovereign God wills two things, affliction and compassion.

God's expressions of pity and his entreaties have heart in them. There is a genuine inclination in God's heart to spare those who have committed treason against his kingdom. But his motivation is complex, and not every true element in it rises to the level of effective choice. In his great and mysterious heart, there are kinds of longings and desires that are real—they tell us something true about his character. Yet not all of these longings govern his actions. He is governed by the depth of his wisdom expressed through a plan that no ordinary human deliberation would ever conceive (Rom. 11:33–36; 1 Cor. 2:9). There are holy and just reasons why the affections of God's heart have the nature, intensity, and proportion that they do.

Objections to the George Washington Illustration

Dabney was aware that several kinds of objections could be raised against the analogy of George Washington as it is applied to God. Three of these are illuminating to consider.

First, someone might say that the analogy works with a human ruler, who is not omnipotent, but not with God, who is almighty. A human ruler foresees negative effects of his pardoning and cannot overcome them, and therefore is constrained to condemn. God is omnipotent, and therefore is not constrained by such inability.

Dabney answers: "We know that [God's] ultimate end is his own glory. But we do not know all the ways in which God may deem his glory is promoted. . . . God may see in his own omniscience, a rational ground other than inability for restraining his actual [inclination] of pity towards a given sinner."[18] Notice how Dabney is not driven by human logic here. He is simply coming to

---

[18] Ibid., 288–9.

terms with Scripture and saying, in effect, "Scripture says that it is this way; therefore, God must have his reasons."

John Calvin on the Simplicity and Unity of God's Will

A second objection to the analogy of George Washington comes from high-level theological reflection on God's unity and simplicity: "Such a theory of motive and free agency may not be applied to the divine will, because of God's absolute simplicity of being, and the unity of his attributes with his essence."[19]

John Calvin saw this problem as well. He was too submitted to the Bible, and too good an exegete, not to notice in the Scriptures what we have been seeing: "In a wonderful and ineffable manner nothing is done without God's will, not even that which is against this will."[20] He gave several biblical examples, such as Eli's sons not obeying their father, "for it was the will of the LORD to put them to death" (1 Sam. 2:25), and Amos 3:6, which says, "Does disaster come to a city, unless the LORD has done it?"

But Calvin took the simplicity and unity of God's essence seriously, so he warned: "God's will is not therefore at war with itself, nor does it change, nor does it pretend not to will what it wills. Even though his will is one and simple in him, it appears manifold to us because, on account of our mental incapacity, we do not grasp how in divers ways it wills and does not will something to take place."[21]

The real issue here is whether God's unity and unchangeableness are jeopardized, and whether he is put at the mercy of creatures who bring about fluctuations in his heart that make him dependent on them and divided in his will. This is the concern when the historic confessions say that God is "without passions." Dabney responds by saying:

---

[19] Ibid., 287.
[20] John Calvin, *Institutes of the Christian Religion*, ed. John T. McNeill, trans. Ford Lewis Battles, Library of Christian Classics, vols. 20–21 (Philadelphia: Westminster, 1960), 235 (I.xviii.3).
[21] Ibid., 234 (I.xviii.3).

While God has no . . . mere susceptibility such that his creature can cause an effect upon it irrespective to God's own will and freedom, yet he has active principles. These are not passions, in the sense of fluctuations or agitations, but nonetheless are they affections of his will, actively distinguished from the cognitions in his intelligence.[22]

Moreover, Dabney says, the actions of his creatures "are real occasions, though not efficient causes, of the action both of the divine affections and will."[23] In other words, God is not at the mercy of his creatures, because, even though he genuinely responds to their actions with affections and choices, this response is always according to his prior willing in complete freedom. Thus, he is not forced to respond by others, and neither is he, as it were, cornered into a frustrated compassion that he did not anticipate.

God's simplicity and unity should not be taken to mean what the Bible forbids that they mean: "The Bible always speaks of God's attributes as distinct, and yet not dividing his unity; of his intelligence and will as different; of his wrath, love, pity, wisdom, as not the same activities of the Infinite Spirit."[24] The unity of God's Spirit lies not in his having no affections or in all his affections being one simple act; rather, his unity lies in the glorious harmony and proportion of all that he is—each affection and propensity revealing something of the unified, harmonious complexity of the infinite mind.

No Agitation in the Divine Mind

The third kind of objection to the analogy of George Washington is an extension of the second, namely, "No such balancing of subjective motives takes place without inward strivings, which would

---

[22] Dabney, "God's Indiscriminate Proposals of Mercy," 291.
[23] Ibid.
[24] Ibid., 290.

be inconsistent with God's immutability and blessedness."[25] Dabney agrees that this is difficult to imagine—that God is moved by all the energy of affections and yet shows all the equanimity of deity. But it is not impossible. He observes wisely that the more pure and steady a person's affections and thoughts are, the less struggle is involved in adjusting them into a rational and righteous decision.

To illustrate, Dabney imagines a man of more unstable condition than the "majestic calmness" of Washington facing the same choice:

> He would have shown far more agitation; he would perhaps have thrown down the pen and snatched it again, and trembled and wept. But this would not have proved a deeper compassion than Washington's. His shallow nature was not capable of such depths of sentiment in any virtuous direction as filled the profounder soul. The cause of the difference would have been in this, that Washington's was a grander and wiser as well as a more feeling soul.[26]

Dabney gives a related illustration of how deep and mixed affections do not have to result in internal strife and agitation:

> Dying saints have sometimes declared that their love for their families was never before so profound and tender; and yet were enabled by dying grace to bid them a final farewell with joyful calmness. If, then, the ennobling of the affections enables the will to adjust the balance between them with less agitation, what will the result be when the wisdom is that of omniscience, the virtue is that of infinite holiness, and the self-command that of omnipotence?[27]

He admits that "no analogy can be perfect between the actions of a finite and the infinite intelligence and will."[28] Yet I think he is

---

[25] Ibid., 287.
[26] Ibid., 298.
[27] Ibid., 299.
[28] Ibid., 287.

right to say that these three objections do not overthrow the essential truth that there can be, in a noble and great heart like George Washington's (even in a divine heart), sincere compassion for a criminal who is nevertheless not set free.

God Is Constrained by His Passion for the Display of the Fullness of His Glory

Therefore, I affirm with John 3:16 and 1 Timothy 2:4 that God loves the world with a real and sincere compassion that desires the salvation of all men.[29] Yet I also affirm that God has chosen from before the foundation of the world those whom he will save from sin. Since not all people are saved, we must choose whether we believe (with the Arminians) that God's will to save all people is restrained by his commitment to ultimate human self-determination or whether we believe (with the Reformed) that God's will to save all people is restrained by his commitment to the glorification of the full range of his perfections in exalting his sovereign grace (Eph. 1:6, 12, 14; Rom. 9:22–23).

This decision should not be made on the basis of philosophical assumptions about what we think human accountability requires. It should be made on the basis of what the Scriptures teach. I do not find in the Bible that human beings have the ultimate power of self-determination. As far as I can tell, this is a philosophical presupposition brought to the Bible rather than found in it.

Christ Invites Everyone to Come—So Should We

My purpose in this book has simply been to show that God's will for all people to be saved is not at odds with the sovereignty of his grace in election, with all the achievements of his grace that flow

[29] For a further support for this in view of unconditional election and particular redemption, see John Piper, "'My Glory I Will Not Give to Another': Preaching the Fullness of Definite Atonement to the Glory of God," in *From Heaven He Came and Sought Her: Definite Atonement in Biblical, Historical, Theological, and Pastoral Perspective*, eds. David Gibson and Jonathan Gibson (Wheaton, IL: Crossway, 2013).

from that election. That is, my answer to the earlier question about what restrains God's will to save all people is his supreme commitment to uphold and display the full range of his glory. His plan from all eternity was to magnify his glory in creation and redemption. He aimed to make the glory of his grace the highest revelation of himself (Eph. 1:6). To that end, he sent his Son into this creation and made Christ—crucified for sinners and conquering death—the climax of the display of the glory of his grace.

With the fullness and the majesty of the achievement of Jesus on the cross as the basis, we now offer him and all that he has achieved for his elect to everyone on earth. Christ invites everyone to come. And everyone who comes is saved. Everyone who receives Christ has been chosen from the foundation of the world and is an heir of an infinite inheritance.

We declare three things as the foundation for the universal offer of the love of God and the salvation of Christ to everyone in the world: (1) Christ really is the all-powerful, all-wise, all-satisfying divine Son of God offered in the gospel; (2) by his death and resurrection, he has acted out God's discriminating, definite electing, regenerating, faith-creating, every-promise-guaranteeing new-covenant love, and thus has purchased and secured irreversibly for his elect everything needed to bring them from deadness in sin to everlasting, glorified life and joy in the presence of God; and (3) everyone, without any exception, who receives Christ as supreme treasure—who believes in his name—will be united to Christ in the embrace of this electing love, and enjoy him and all his gifts forever.[30]

Therefore, I say with the last chapter of the Bible: "Let the one who is thirsty come; let the one who desires take the water of life without price" (Rev. 22:17).

---

[30] These three points are adapted from my chapter, "'My Glory I Will Not Give to Another': Preaching the Fullness of Definite Atonement to the Glory of God."

Acknowledgments

Thank you to Multnomah Books and Baker Publishing Group for previously publishing the substance of this book. The first version appeared as an essay in *The Grace of God, the Bondage of the Will: Biblical and Practical Perspectives on Calvinism*, edited by Thomas R. Schreiner and Bruce A. Ware (Baker, 1995), and was republished in *Still Sovereign: Contemporary Perspectives on Election, Foreknowledge, and Grace*, edited by Schreiner and Ware (Baker, 2000). Then it became an appendix in John Piper, *The Pleasures of God: Meditations on God's Delight in Being God*, revised edition (Multnomah, 2000). The 2012 third revised edition of *The Pleasures of God* did not include this essay, and that opened the way for it to be revised and expanded for republication here.

And thank you to David Mathis, executive editor at Desiring God, for navigating these publishing waters for me and shepherding this book from one form to another.

The biblical, exegetical, and intellectual debts I owe are reflected especially in the footnotes. But there are always more debts to be paid than one can mention. In one sense, as Paul said, we are debtors to everyone (Rom. 1:14). It is especially fitting to say this in a book devoted to advancing the evangelistic and missionary cause of inviting everyone to come to Christ. I am happy to be such a debtor.

As I write this, I have just finished thirty-three years as a pastor of Bethlehem Baptist Church in Minneapolis, Minnesota. I want to say again how thankful I am for the support of this people for my writing during all those years. This book is the fruit of that pastoral ministry.

My life as pastor and writer would be unthinkable without my wife, Noël. She is woven into everything I am and do. I thank God for her.

My prayer is that this book would empower thousands to proclaim the unsearchable riches of Christ and "that repentance and forgiveness of sins should be proclaimed in his name to all nations" (Luke 24:47).

⚜ desiring God

If you would like to explore further the vision of God and life presented in this book, we at Desiring God would love to serve you. We have thousands of resources to help you grow in your passion for Jesus Christ and help you spread that passion to others. At desiringGod.org, you'll find almost everything John Piper has written and preached, including more than sixty books. We've made over thirty years of his sermons available free online for you to read, listen to, download, and watch.

In addition, you can access hundreds of articles, find out where John Piper is speaking, and learn about our conferences. Desiring God has a whatever-you-can-afford policy, designed for individuals with limited discretionary funds. If you'd like more information about this policy, please contact us at the address or phone number below. We exist to help you treasure Jesus and his gospel above all things because *he is most glorified in you when you are most satisfied in him.* Let us know how we can serve you!

Desiring God
Post Office Box 2901 / Minneapolis, Minnesota 55402
888.346.4700   mail@desiringGod.org

Scripture Index